Vegetarian Recipes

By
BookSumo Press
All rights reserved

Published by
http://www.booksumo.com

ENJOY THE RECIPES?

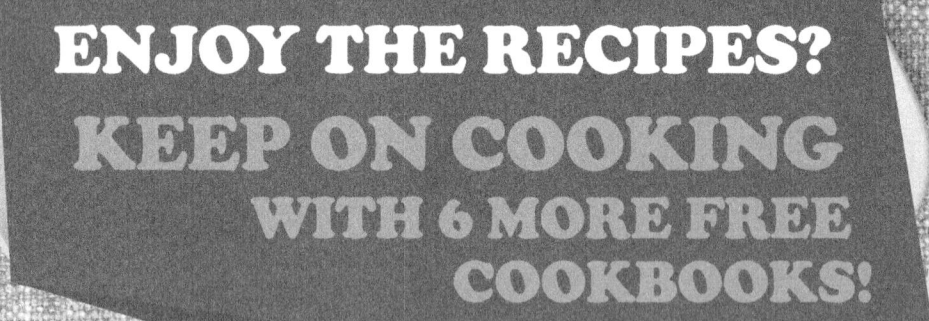

KEEP ON COOKING WITH 6 MORE FREE COOKBOOKS!

Visit our website and simply enter your email address to join the club and receive your 6 cookbooks.

http://booksumo.com/magnet

https://www.instagram.com/booksumopress/

https://www.facebook.com/booksumo/

LEGAL NOTES

All Rights Reserved. No Part Of This Book May Be Reproduced Or Transmitted In Any Form Or By Any Means. Photocopying, Posting Online, And / Or Digital Copying Is Strictly Prohibited Unless Written Permission Is Granted By The Book's Publishing Company. Limited Use Of The Book's Text Is Permitted For Use In Reviews Written For The Public.

Table of Contents

Herbed Fava Beans 9

Sesame Burgers 10

Cajun Burgers with Lemon Sauce 11

Oregon Inspired Burgers 12

Cereal Mayo Burgers 14

Asian Italian Burgers with Cajun Mayo 15

London Shiitake Worcestershire Burgers 16

Portobello Pepperjack Monterey Spicy Burgers 17

Eggplant Patties with Cheddar 18

Horseradish Mushroom Burger I 19

Zucchini Burgers 20

Microwave Broccoli Curry 21

Saturday Night Curry 22

October's Apple Curry 23

Lunch Box Soup Curry 24

Whole Grain Curry 25

Vegetarian Curry Japanese Style 26

Curry Salad 28

South East Asian All Ingredient Curry 29

Punjabi Greens Curry 30

Easy Veggie Curry Soup from Vietnam 31

Vegetarian Curry Sri Lankan Style 32

Peanut Thai Curry 33

Okra from Afghanistan 34

North Indian Curried Okra 35

Summer-Time Charred Okra 36

Barbados Style Okras 37

Louisiana Okra 38

Andhra Style Okra Stir-Fry 39

Southern Okra and Grits Fritters 40

South Carolina Deep Fried Okra 41

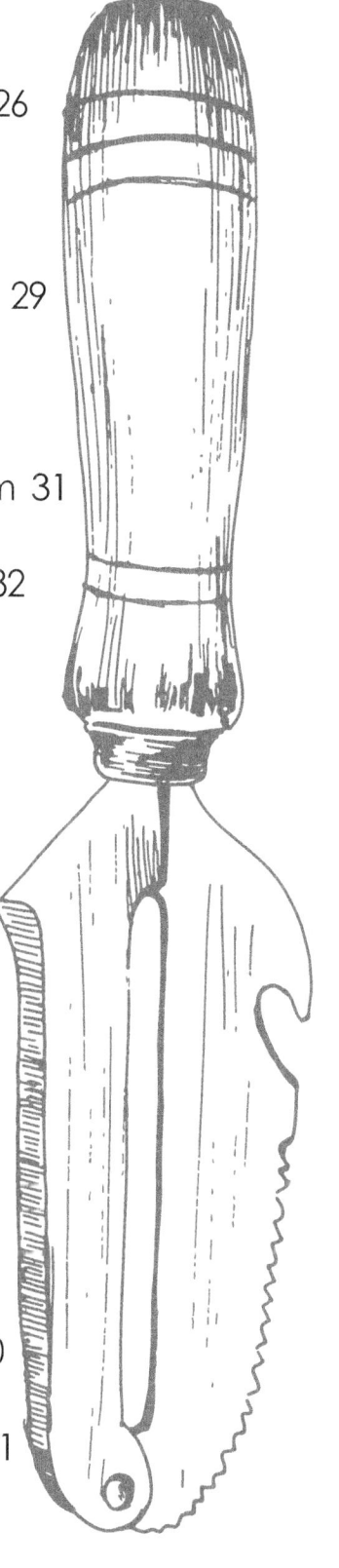

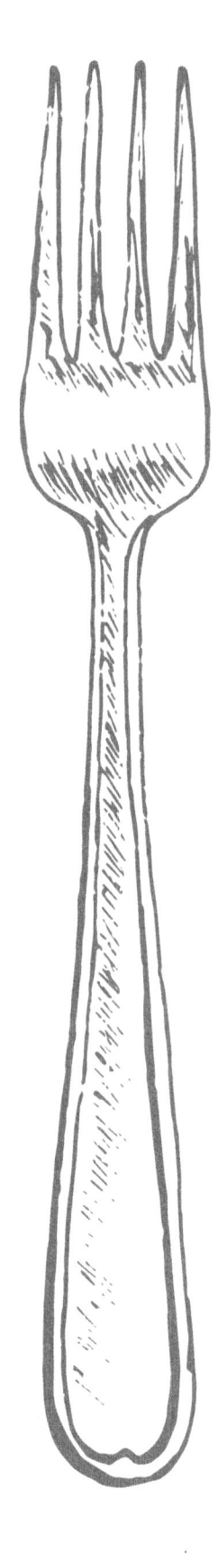

Okra Burgers 42

Baton Rouge Vegetarian Gumbo 43

Spring Veggies Fiesta 44

Zesty Veggies Roast 45

Cherry Potato Roast Salad 46

Rosemary Roasted Rooty Veggies 47

Baby Herbed Veggies Roast 48

Crunchy Roasted Veggies Pie 49

Egg Salad 50

Amish Pasta Salad 51

Elegant Cucumber Salad 52

Cashew Salad 53

Almond Salad I 54

Maggie's Favorite Easy Rigatoni 55

Cannellini Classic 56

Pasta Rustic 57

Simple Sundried Tomato Pasta 58

A Light Thai Inspired Pasta 59

Easy Mushroom Pasta 60

Garden Lasagna III 61

Garbanzos and Basil Tofu 62

Easy BBQ Tofu 63

Easy BBQ Tofu II 64

Orange Chili Carrot Tofu 65

Rustic Tofu 66

Cheddar Tofu Quiche I 67

Celery Tofu Salad 68

Creamy Asiago Tofu 69

Mexican Style Tofu 70

Lasagna II 71

Sweet Tofu Stir Fry 72

American Style Tofu 73

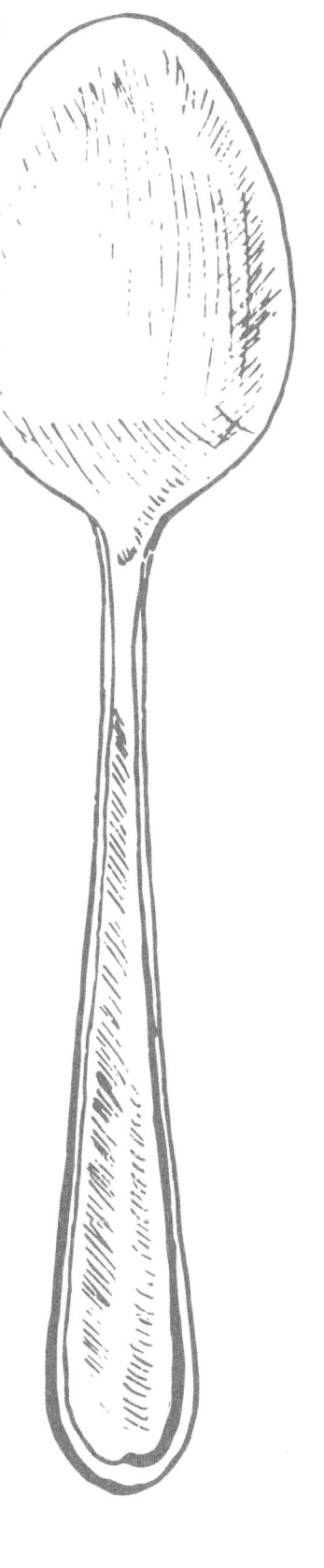

Indian Style Tofu 74

Cilantro and Sesame Tofu 75

Tofu Party Dip 76

Traditional Indian Curry Paste 77

Simple Homemade Red / Green Curry Paste 78

Herbed Fava Beans

Prep Time: 15 mins
Total Time: 20 mins

Servings per Recipe: 4
Calories   144.9
Fat   5.5g
Cholesterol   7.6mg
Sodium   27.8mg
Carbohydrates   17.9g
Protein   6.8g

Ingredients

- 12 oz. frozen fava beans
- 1 tbsp butter
- 4 -5 scallions, sliced
- 1 tbsp chopped fresh cilantro
- 1 tsp chopped of fresh mint
- 1/2-1 tsp ground cumin
- 2 tsps olive oil
- salt

Directions

1. In a pan of water, cook the fava beans for about 3-4 minutes and drain well.
2. Keep aside to cool.
3. Peel off the outer skin of the fava beans and keep aside.
4. In a pan, melt the butter and sauté the scallions for about 2-3 minutes.
5. Stir in the fava beans, fresh herbs and a pinch of salt.
6. Stir in the olive oil and remove it from heat.
7. Serve immediately.

SESAME Burgers

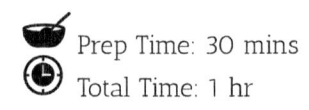

🥣 Prep Time: 30 mins
🕐 Total Time: 1 hr

Servings per Recipe: 4
Calories   186.4
Fat   3.0g
Cholesterol   0.0mg
Sodium   352.6mg
Carbohydrates   29.4g
Protein   11.9g

Ingredients

1 (15 ounce) cans cannellini, rinsed and drained
1/3 C. chopped onion (I use the frozen kind thawed out, this'd be one small onion)
2 garlic cloves, peeled
1 tbsp fresh parsley, chopped (or 1 tsp dried parsley)
2 tbsps nutritional yeast
2 tbsps sesame seeds (not tahini)

2 egg whites (or 1 whole egg)
1/2 C. breadcrumbs (I use whole-wheat)
1 tsp paprika
1/2 tsp sea salt
1/2 tsp black pepper
1 dash cayenne pepper

Directions

1. Wash the beans with some fresh water. Place it in a colander to get remove the water.
2. Get a food processor: Add the beans with rest of the ingredients. Pulse them several times until they become smooth. Transfer the mix into a bowl and cover it.
3. Place it in the fridge for 45 min. Shape the mix into 4 burgers.
4. Place a large skillet on medium heat. Heat the sesame oil in it. Add the burgers and cook them for 8 min on each side. Assemble your burgers with your favorite toppings.
5. Serve them right away.
6. Enjoy.

Cajun Burgers with Lemon Sauce

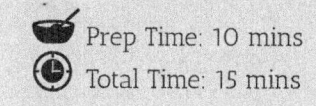

Prep Time: 10 mins
Total Time: 15 mins

Servings per Recipe: 4
Calories   246.9
Fat   6.5g
Cholesterol   56.6mg
Sodium   1130.1mg
Carbohydrates   35.9g
Protein   112.8g

Ingredients

1 (15 ounce) cans cannellini beans (drain liquid) or 1 (15 ounce) cans chickpeas (drain liquid)
1 egg
1 onion
Approximately 1/2 C. breadcrumbs, crushed crackers or flour
1 tbsp minced garlic
Salt and pepper
1 tbsp cumin (optional)
Nonstick cooking spray
SEASONINGS (FEEL FREE TO MIX AND MATCH)
Curry powder
Garam masala
Smoked paprika
Minced chipotle pepper
Cayenne
Oregano
Cajun seasoning
Cheese
SAUCE
1/4 C. mayonnaise
2 - 3 tbsps lemon juice
1 tbsp garlic powder or 1 tbsp minces garlic
1 chipotle pepper, minced (optional)

Directions

1. Get a small bowl: Add the sauce ingredients. Whisk them well. Place the sauce in the fridge.
2. Get a food processor: Add the garlic, onion bean and seasonings mix. Pulse them several times until they become finely chopped.
3. Add the breadcrumbs with egg and flour. Mix them well. Shape the mix into 4 burgers.
4. Place a large skillet on medium heat. Heat the sesame oil in it. Add the burgers and cook them for 8 min on each side. Assemble your burgers with the lemon sauce and your favorite toppings.
5. Serve them right away.
6. Enjoy.

OREGON INSPIRED
Burgers

Prep Time: 1 hr
Total Time: 1 hr 15 mins

Servings per Recipe: 12
Calories 149.8
Fat 1.9g
Cholesterol 0.0mg
Sodium 250.0mg
Carbohydrates 28.5g
Protein 4.4g

Ingredients

BASE
4 C. water (divided into 2 C. each)
1 C. lentils (DO NOT SOAK AHEAD OF TIME!)
1 C. black rice
1/4 tsp salt
1 tbsp olive oil
FORMING STAGE
3/4 C. flour
1 tsp minced garlic (2 cloves, mashed and minced but I use the liquid stuff)
1 tsp kosher salt (or sea salt)
2 tsp tahini
DRY SEASONING
3/4 tsp paprika
1/2 tsp onion powder
1/4 tsp black pepper
1/4 tsp cayenne

1/4 tsp mustard (dry powdered mustard, not wet)
1 dash oregano
VEGGIES
1/4 C. peas
1/4 C. carrot
1/4 C. broccoli (I used the very fine chopped broccoli from the freezer section, florets are too big)
1/4 C. corn
THROW IN AT THE END
1/2 C. flour

Directions

1. Before you do anything preheat the oven to 350 F. Grease a baking sheet.
2. Cook the rice according to the directions on the package. Cook the lentils according to the directions on the package.
3. Get a mixing bowl: Add the rice and lentils. Press them with a fork until they become slightly mashed. Add the garlic, kosher salt, and tahini. Mix them well.
4. Stir in the flour gradually followed by the seasonings, veggies and the rest of the flour while mixing all the time. Place it aside for 12 min.

5. Shape the mix into 12 burgers. Place them on the baking sheet. Cook them in the oven 16 min. Assemble your burgers with your favorite toppings. Serve them right away.
6. Enjoy.

CEREAL
Mayo Burgers

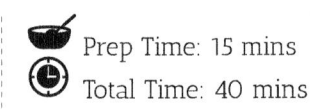

Prep Time: 15 mins
Total Time: 40 mins

Servings per Recipe: 12
Calories   206 kcal
Fat   11.5 g
Carbohydrates   122.5g
Protein   4.1 g
Cholesterol   34 mg
Sodium   300 mg

Ingredients

- 2 C. shredded carrots
- 2 eggs
- 1/2 C. mayonnaise
- 1 medium onion, minced
- 2 tbsps olive oil
- 1 clove garlic, chopped
- Salt and pepper to taste
- 6 C. soft bread crumbs
- 4 C. whole wheat flake cereal, crumbled

Directions

1. Before you do anything preheat the oven to 375 F. Line up a baking sheet.
2. Get a heatproof bowl: Add the carrot and microwave it for 4 min.
3. Get a mixing bowl: Add the eggs, mayonnaise, onion, olive oil, garlic, salt, pepper, and carrots. Mix them well. Add the breadcrumbs and mix them again. Form the mix into 12 cakes.
4. Place the cereal in a shallow pate. Coat the burgers with the cereal. Place the cakes in the baking sheet. Cook the burgers in the oven for 14 min. Flip them and cook them for another 14 min.
5. Assemble your burgers with your favorite toppings. Serve them right away.
6. Enjoy.

Asian Italian Burgers with Cajun Mayo

🥣 Prep Time: 15 mins
🕐 Total Time: 2 hrs 40 mins

Servings per Recipe: 4
Calories   375 kcal
Fat   22.5 g
Carbohydrates   337.8g
Protein   7.1 g
Cholesterol   21 mg
Sodium   2459 mg

Ingredients

- 4 large mushroom caps
- 1/2 C. soy sauce
- 1/2 C. Italian dressing
- 4 cloves garlic, chopped, or more to taste
- 1 large red bell pepper
- 1 C. reduced-fat mayonnaise
- 1 tbsp Cajun spice, or to taste
- 2 tbsp sriracha
- 4 hamburger buns split

Directions

1. Get a zip lock bag: Add the mushroom with soy sauce, Italian dressing, and garlic. Shake the bag roughly to coat the ingredients. Place it aside for 2 h 30 min.
2. Before you do anything heat the grill and grease it.
3. Cook the bell pepper for 6 min on each side. Drain the mushroom caps from the marinade and cook them for 7 min on each side.
4. Transfer the bell pepper to a zip lock bag and seal it and place them aside for 5 min sweat. Peel the bell peppers and chop them.
5. Get a mixing bowl: Add the roasted bell pepper with mayo and Cajun spice. Mix them well. Place it in the fridge until ready to serve.
6. Assemble your burgers with your favorite toppings then add an even amount of Sriracha to each. Serve them right away.
7. Enjoy.

LONDON
Shiitake Worcestershire Burgers

Prep Time: 20 mins
Total Time: 30 mins

Servings per Recipe: 6
Calories   54.5
Fat   0.5g
Cholesterol   0.0mg
Sodium   65.6mg
Carbohydrates   9.1g
Protein   4.4g

Ingredients

1 lb. fresh shiitake mushrooms, about 6 C. chopped finely
1 large onion, minced
2 slices white bread, finely diced
2 tbsps Worcestershire sauce
2 egg whites or 1 egg
Salt
Ground black pepper

Directions

1. Place a large skillet on medium heat. Grease it with oil or cooking spray. Add the onion with mushroom and sauté them for 6 min. Add the bread dices with Worcestershire sauce. Sauté them for 1 min
2. Turn off the heat. Place the mix aside to lose heat.
3. Get a mixing bowl: Add the eggs and mix them well. Add the onion mix with salt and pepper. Mix them well. Shape the mix into 6 burgers.
4. Place a large skillet on medium heat. Heat in it a splash of oil. Add the burgers and cook them for 8 min on each side.
5. Assemble your burgers with your favorite toppings. Serve them right away.
6. Enjoy

Portobello Pepperjack Monterey Spicy Burgers

Prep Time: 15 mins
Total Time: 35 mins

Servings per Recipe: 4
Calories   203 kcal
Fat   14.6 g
Carbohydrates   9.8 g
Protein   10.3 g
Cholesterol   20 mg
Sodium   259 mg

Ingredients

4 Portobello mushroom caps
1/4 C. balsamic vinegar
2 tbsps olive oil
1 tsp dried basil
1 tsp dried oregano
1 tbsp minced garlic
Salt and pepper to taste

4 (1 ounce) slices Pepperjack cheese
4 slices Monterey cheese
1 tbsp diced jalapeno from a jar

Directions

1. Before you do anything heat the grill and grease it.
2. Get a mixing bowl: Add the vinegar, oil, basil, oregano, garlic, salt, and pepper. Mix them well to make the marinade.
3. Stir the mushroom into the marinade. Place it aside for 18 min. Drain the mushroom and place the marinade aside.
4. Cook the mushroom caps on the grill for 7 min on each side while basting them with the marinade every 2 min. Place the cheese slices on the mushroom while it is hot to melt.
5. Assemble your burgers with your favorite toppings. Then evenly divide the diced jalapeno amongst the burgers.
6. Enjoy.

EGGPLANT Patties with Cheddar

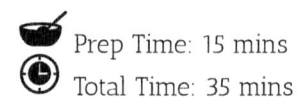

Prep Time: 15 mins
Total Time: 35 mins

Servings per Recipe: 6
Calories   266 kcal
Fat   14.4 g
Carbohydrates   23.6 g
Protein   12.4 g
Cholesterol   86 mg
Sodium   911 mg

Ingredients

- 2 medium eggplants, peeled and cubed
- 1 C. shredded sharp Cheddar cheese
- 1 C. Italian seasoned bread crumbs
- 2 eggs, beaten
- 2 tbsps dried parsley
- 2 tbsps chopped onion
- 1 clove garlic, minced
- 1 C. vegetable oil for frying
- 1 tsp salt
- 1/2 tsp ground black pepper

Directions

1. For 4 mins cook all the eggplants in the microwave on medium. Then flip the eggplants and cook for another 3 mins.
2. Remove any resulting juices and mash the eggplants together.
3. Add the following to the mashed eggplant: salt, cheese, garlic, bread crumbs, onions, parsley, and eggs.
4. Now take your mix, and with your hands form as many patties as possible.
5. For 6 mins per side cook the patties in hot oil.
6. Enjoy on a bun, hamburger style.

Horseradish Mushroom Burger I

Prep Time: 5 mins
Total Time: 20 mins

Servings per Recipe: 2
Calories   313 kcal
Fat   15.3 g
Carbohydrates 29.9 g
Protein   15.5 g
Cholesterol   53 mg
Sodium   934 mg

Ingredients

- 2 Portobello mushroom caps
- 3 tsps horseradish sauce
- 2 leaves romaine lettuce
- 2 slices tomato
- 2 hamburger buns

Directions

1. Cover a baking sheet with foil and then coat it with nonstick spray before setting your oven to 450 degrees before doing anything else.
2. Cut the stem of your mushrooms off and then clean them under water.
3. Now put the mushrooms on your baking sheet and cook them in the oven for 20 mins.
4. Coat each of your buns with 1.5 tsps of horseradish and then a piece of tomato and lettuce on one bun. Top the other bun with a mushroom cap and form a burger.
5. Enjoy.

ZUCCHINI
Burgers

Prep Time: 10 mins
Total Time: 30 mins

Servings per Recipe: 4
Calories   245 kcal
Fat   14.7 g
Carbohydrates   15.7g
Protein   12.8 g
Cholesterol   111 mg
Sodium   282 mg

Ingredients

- 2 C. grated zucchini
- 2 eggs, beaten
- 1/4 C. diced onion
- 1/2 C. all-purpose flour
- 1/2 C. grated Parmesan cheese
- 1/2 C. shredded mozzarella cheese
- salt to taste
- 2 tbsps vegetable oil

Directions

1. Get a bowl, combine: salt, zucchini, mozzarella, eggs, parmesan, flour, and onions.
2. Combine the mix then get your oil hot.
3. Once the veggie oil is hot, fry large dollops of the mix, until it is browned on both sides.
4. Enjoy.

Microwave Broccoli Curry

Prep Time: 15 mins
Total Time: 25 mins

Servings per Recipe: 4
Calories	235.9
Fat	10 g
Cholesterol	0 mg
Sodium	665.8 mg
Carbohydrates	30.3 g
Protein	8.7 g

Ingredients

- 1 onion, sliced
- 2 tbsp red curry paste, see appendix
- 3 C. broccoli, sliced
- 1 (400 g) can chickpeas, drained
- 1 C. light coconut milk
- 1 tbsp lemon juice
- 1 tbsp soy sauce
- 1/2 C. nuts, chopped

Directions

1. In a large microwave safe casserole dish, place the onion and curry paste and cook on Very High for about 2 minutes.
2. Add the broccoli, chick peas, coconut milk, lemon juice and soy sauce and cook on Very High for about 6-8 minutes.
3. Serve over the jasmine rice with a garnishing of the nuts.

SATURDAY NIGHT Curry

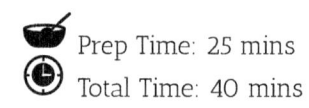

Prep Time: 25 mins
Total Time: 40 mins

Servings per Recipe: 6
Calories   232 kcal
Fat   13.2 g
Carbohydrates   16.9 g
Protein   16.5 g
Cholesterol   0 mg
Sodium   680 mg

Ingredients

2 bunches green onions
1 (14 oz.) can light coconut milk
1/4 C. soy sauce, divided
1/2 tsp brown sugar
1 1/2 tsp curry powder
1 tsp minced fresh ginger
2 tsp chili paste
1 lb. firm tofu, cut into 3/4 inch cubes
4 roma (plum) tomatoes, chopped
1 yellow bell pepper, thinly sliced
4 oz. fresh mushrooms, chopped
1/4 C. chopped fresh basil
4 C. chopped bok choy
salt to taste

Directions

1. Chop the white parts of the green onions finely.
2. Chop the green parts of the green onions into 2-inch pieces.
3. In a large heavy skillet, mix together the coconut milk, 3 tbsp of the soy sauce, brown sugar, curry powder, ginger and chili paste and bring to a boil.
4. Stir in the tofu, tomatoes, yellow pepper, mushrooms and white part of the green onions and cook, covered for about 5 minutes, stirring occasionally.
5. Stir in the basil, bok choy, salt and remaining soy sauce and cook for about 5 minutes.
6. Serve with a garnishing of the green parts of the green onion.

October's Apple Curry

🍲 Prep Time: 30 mins
🕐 Total Time: 2 hrs 10 mins

Servings per Recipe: 6
Calories   360 kcal
Fat   3.7 g
Carbohydrates   64.3g
Protein   20.1 g
Cholesterol   0 mg
Sodium   244 mg

Ingredients

1 C. red lentils
1 C. brown lentils
8 C. water
1/2 tsp turmeric
1 tbsp canola oil
1 large onion, diced
2 tomatoes, cored and chopped
3 cloves garlic, minced
1 1/2 tbsp curry powder
2 tsp ground cumin

1/2 tsp salt
1/2 tsp black pepper
1/4 tsp ground cloves
2 C. peeled, cubed (1-inch), seeded pumpkin
2 potatoes, unpeeled and chopped
2 carrots, peeled and diced
2 C. packed fresh spinach, chopped
1 Granny Smith apple, unpeeled, cored and diced

Directions

1. In a pan, add the both lentils, water and turmeric on medium-low heat and cook for about 45 minutes.
2. Drain well, reserving 2 1/2 C. of the cooking liquid.
3. Meanwhile in a large deep pan, heat the canola oil on medium heat and sauté the onion for about 5 minutes.
4. Stir in the tomatoes and garlic and cook for about 5 minutes, stirring occasionally.
5. Stir in the curry powder, cumin, salt, pepper and cloves.
6. Increase the heat to medium-low and stir in the cooked lentil, reserved cooking liquid, pumpkin, potatoes and carrots and simmer, covered for about 35-45 minutes.
7. Stir in the spinach and apple and simmer for about 15 minutes.

LUNCH BOX
Soup Curry

Prep Time: 15 mins
Total Time: 40 mins

Servings per Recipe: 6
Calories   133 kcal
Fat   5.4 g
Carbohydrates   20.2g
Protein   2.4 g
Cholesterol   0 mg
Sodium   415 mg

Ingredients

2 tbsp vegetable oil
1 onion, chopped
1 tbsp curry powder
2 lb. carrots, chopped

4 C. vegetable broth
2 C. water

Directions

1. In a large pan, heat the oil on medium heat and sauté the onion till tender.
2. Stir in the curry powder.
3. Add the chopped carrots and stir to combine well.
4. Add the vegetable broth and simmer for about 20 minutes.
5. Remove from the heat and keep aside to cool slightly.
6. Transfer the soup mixture into a blender and pulse till smooth.
7. Return the soup in the pan and, add enough water to thin according to your required consistency.
8. Cook till heated completely before serving.

Whole Grain Curry

Prep Time: 10 mins
Total Time: 8 hrs 40 mins

Servings per Recipe: 4
Calories	278 kcal
Fat	9.1 g
Carbohydrates	42.9 g
Protein	6.4 g
Cholesterol	0 mg
Sodium	592 mg

Ingredients

- 1 C. millet
- 2 tbsp olive oil
- 1 onion, diced
- 2 cloves garlic, diced
- 2 1/2 C. water
- 1 tsp salt
- 1/2 tsp ground cumin
- 2 tsp curry powder

Directions

1. In a large bowl of the water, soak the millet for about 8 hours to overnight.
2. Drain the millet completely.
3. In a large skillet, heat the oil on medium heat and sauté the onion and garlic for about 10-15 minutes.
4. Stir in the millet, 2 1/2 C. of the water, salt and cumin and simmer, covered for about 20 minutes.
5. Stir in the curry powder and remove from the heat.

VEGETARIAN CURRY
Japanese Style

Prep Time: 30 mins
Total Time: 1 hr

Servings per Recipe: 2
Calories	297 kcal
Fat	11.6 g
Carbohydrates	45.1g
Protein	8 g
Cholesterol	0 mg
Sodium	236 mg

Ingredients

2 C. cubed Japanese turnips
1 potato, peeled and cubed
1 tomato, diced
1 C. water
1/4 tsp ground turmeric
Spice Paste:
1 tsp canola oil
2 dried red chilis
2 small Thai green chilis
1 (1/2 inch) piece cinnamon stick
4 pearl onions
2 tbsp unsweetened dried coconut
1 tbsp coriander seeds
5 cashews
2 green cardamom pods
2 whole cloves

1/2 tsp fennel seeds
1/4 tsp cumin seeds
2 tbsp chopped cilantro
2 tbsp chopped fresh mint
1 tsp water, or as needed
1 tsp canola oil
1/2 tsp fennel seeds
1 (1 inch) piece cinnamon stick
2 cloves garlic, minced
1 (1 inch) piece fresh ginger root, minced
4 fresh curry leaves
1/4 C. peas
1 pinch salt

Directions

1. In a large pan, add the turnips, potato, diced tomato, 1 C. of the water and turmeric and bring to a boil.
2. Reduce the heat and simmer for about 15 minutes.
3. In a skillet, heat 1 tsp of the canola oil on medium heat and sauté the chilis, 1/2-inch piece of the cinnamon stick, pearl onions, coconut, coriander, cashews, cardamom pods, cloves, 1/2 tsp of the fennel seeds and cumin seeds for about 3 minutes.
4. Remove from the heat and transfer into a spice grinder.
5. Add the cilantro, mint and 1 tsp of the water and grind till a smooth paste forms.
6. In a large skillet, heat 1 tsp of the canola oil on medium-low heat and sauté 1/2 tsp of the

fennel seeds and 1-inch piece of the cinnamon stick for about 30 seconds.
7. Add the minced garlic, ginger and curry leaves and sauté for about 2 minutes.
8. Add the cooked vegetables and spice paste and bring to a boil. (Add more water if curry becomes too thick.)
9. Stir in the green peas and salt.
10. Reduce the heat and simmer for about 10 minutes.

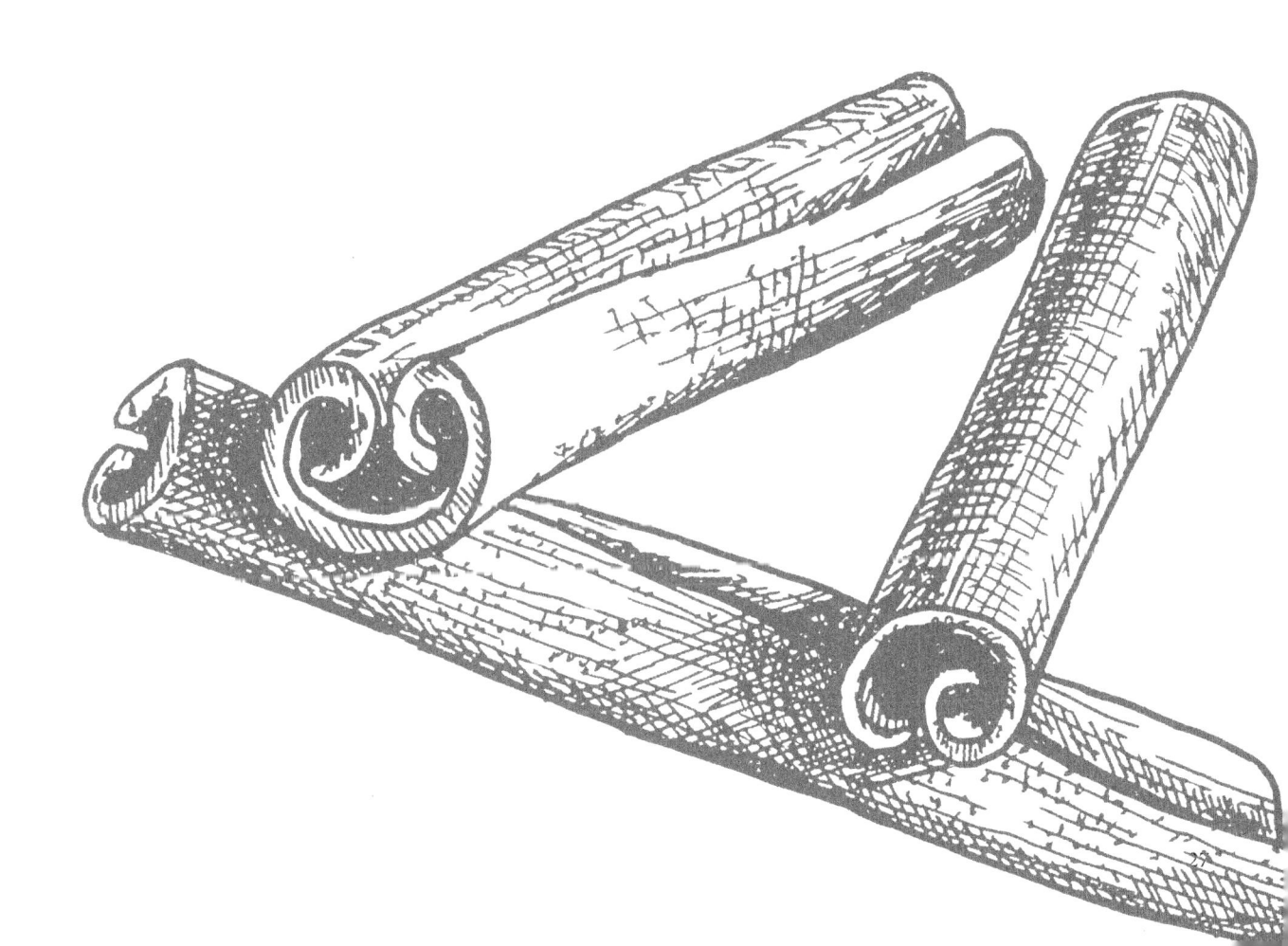

CURRY
Salad

🥣 Prep Time: 20 mins
🕐 Total Time: 20 mins

Servings per Recipe: 2
Calories   292 kcal
Fat   16.3 g
Carbohydrates   40.4g
Protein   3 g
Cholesterol   0 mg
Sodium   127 mg

Ingredients

1 sweet apple, grated
2 carrots, grated
1/4 C. raisins
2 tbsp chopped fresh parsley
Dressing:
1 lemon, juiced
2 tbsp olive oil

1 tbsp toasted sesame seeds
1 tsp curry powder
1/2 tsp maple syrup
salt and ground black pepper to taste

Directions

1. In a large bowl, mix together the apple, carrots, raisins and parsley.
2. In a container with a tight-fitting lid, mix together the remaining ingredients.
3. Cover the jar tightly and shake till well combined.
4. Place the dressing over the salad and mix till well combined.

South East Asian
All Ingredient Curry

Prep Time: 20 mins
Total Time: 1 hr 2 mins

Servings per Recipe: 4
Calories   765 kcal
Fat   38.5 g
Carbohydrates   90.6 g
Protein   20.6 g
Cholesterol   0 mg
Sodium   749 mg

Ingredients

Brown Rice:
3 C. water
2 C. brown rice
1 tbsp soy sauce
1/2 tsp salt
Panang Curry:
1 tbsp vegetable oil
2 1/2 tbsp red curry paste, see appendix
1 (14 oz.) can coconut milk
1 tbsp vegetarian fish sauce

1 tbsp white sugar
5 kaffir lime leaves
8 oz. fried tofu, cubed
2 C. broccoli florets
1/2 red bell pepper, chopped into 1-inch pieces
1/4 C. diagonally sliced carrots

Directions

1. In a rice cooker, mix together the water, brown rice, soy sauce and salt.
2. Cook, covered about 35 minutes according to manufacturer's directions.
3. In a wide skillet, heat the vegetable oil on medium heat and sauté the curry paste for about 1-2 minutes.
4. Add the coconut milk, fish sauce, white sugar and lime leaves and stir to combine.
5. Reduce the heat to medium-low and simmer, covered for about 5 minutes.
6. Stir in the tofu, broccoli, red bell pepper and carrots and simmer for about 1-2 minutes.
7. Serve this curry over the cooked brown rice.

PUNJABI
Greens Curry

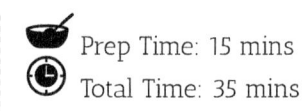

🍲 Prep Time: 15 mins
🕐 Total Time: 35 mins

Servings per Recipe: 2
Calories	333 kcal
Fat	20.1 g
Carbohydrates	22.7g
Protein	18.9 g
Cholesterol	17 mg
Sodium	7499 mg

Ingredients

- 2 tbsp vegetable oil, divided
- 2 C. chopped fresh spinach
- 1 tsp ground cumin
- 3/4 C. chopped onion
- 2 green chili peppers, chopped
- 2 tsp chopped garlic
- 2 tomatoes, chopped
- 1/2 C. water
- 2 tsp ground coriander
- 1 tsp ground red chilis
- 2 tbsp salt
- 8 oz. paneer, cubed

Directions

1. In a skillet, heat 1 tbsp of the vegetable oil on medium heat and cook the spinach for about 3-4 minutes.
2. Remove from the heat and keep aside to cool slightly.
3. Transfer the spinach into a food processor and pulse till a rough paste forms.
4. In a pan, heat the remaining 1 tbsp of the oil on medium heat and sauté the cumin for about 30 seconds.
5. Add the onion, green chili peppers and garlic and sauté for about 3-4 minutes.
6. Stir in the tomatoes and simmer, covered for about 1 minute.
7. Add the spinach paste, water, ground coriander, red chili powder and salt and cook for about 2-3 minutes.
8. Stir in the paneer and simmer for about 1-2 minutes more.

Easy Veggie Curry Soup from Vietnam

Prep Time: 20 mins
Total Time: 37 mins

Servings per Recipe: 4
Calories   264 kcal
Fat   22.1 g
Carbohydrates   16.4g
Protein   6.1 g
Cholesterol   6 mg
Sodium   1331 mg

Ingredients

1/2 onion, diced
2 1/2 tbsp curry powder
1 (32 fluid oz.) container vegetable broth
1/2 lemon, sliced
1 1/4-inch-thick slices fresh ginger, peeled
1 1/2 tsp white sugar
salt to taste
1 lb. assorted mushrooms
1 (13.5 oz.) can coconut milk
1 tbsp fresh lemon juice
salt to taste
8 kaffir lime leaves

Directions

1. Heat a greased pan on high heat and sauté the onion for about 2 minutes.
2. Stir in the curry powder.
3. Add the vegetable broth, lemon, ginger, sugar and salt and stir to combine.
4. Reduce the heat to medium and cook for about 2-3 minutes.
5. Stir in the mushrooms and cook for about 3 minutes.
6. Stir in in the coconut milk and lemon juice and remove from the heat.
7. Stir in the lime leaves and keep aside for about 5 minutes.
8. Discard the lime leaves before serving.

VEGETARIAN CURRY
Sri Lankan Style

Prep Time: 20 mins
Total Time: 35 mins

Servings per Recipe: 4
Calories   381 kcal
Fat   9.8 g
Carbohydrates   67.9g
Protein   8.6 g
Cholesterol   8 mg
Sodium   609 mg

Ingredients

3/4 tsp coriander seed
1/4 tsp fennel seed
1/4 tsp cumin seed
4 leaves fresh curry
4 large potatoes - peeled and cubed
1 tbsp ghee (clarified butter)
1/2 onion, finely chopped
1 clove garlic, minced

1 (1 inch) piece fresh ginger root, grated
1/2 tsp cumin seed
1/2 tsp coriander seed
1/2 C. coconut milk
1 tbsp chopped fresh cilantro
salt to taste

Directions

1. For the fresh curry powder, in a small skillet, dry roast the 3/4 tsp of the coriander, 1/4 tsp of the fennel, and 1/4 tsp of the cumin seeds individually till aromatic.
2. In the same skillet, mix together all the roasted spices and curry leaves on low heat and dry roast for about 5 minutes more.
3. With a mortar and pestle, grind the spices and curry leaves.
4. Now, with the mortar and pestle, grind the remaining coriander and cumin seeds.
5. In a microwave safe bowl, place the potato cubes and microwave for about 3-5 minutes.
6. In a large skillet, melt the ghee on medium heat and sauté the onion, garlic and ginger till golden and aromatic.
7. Add the cumin and coriander seeds powder and fresh curry powder and sauté for about 30 seconds.
8. Stir in the potatoes and cook for about 3 minutes.
9. Stir in the coconut milk and bring to a gentle boil.
10. Reduce the heat to low and simmer, covered for about 7 minutes.
11. Stir in the salt and remove from the heat.
12. Serve with a topping of the chopped fresh cilantro.

Peanut Thai Curry

Prep Time: 5 mins
Total Time: 30 mins

Servings per Recipe: 6
Calories	581 kcal
Fat	22.8 g
Carbohydrates	79.3g
Protein	16.4 g
Cholesterol	0 mg
Sodium	1078 mg

Ingredients

- 1 1/2 C. white rice
- 3 C. water
- 1 (14 oz.) can coconut milk
- 5 tbsp peanut butter
- 2 (14.5 oz.) cans chickpeas (garbanzo beans), rinsed and drained
- 2 tsp ground ginger
- 1/8 tsp ground cinnamon
- 1/8 tsp cayenne pepper
- 1 (28 oz.) can diced tomatoes, drained
- 1 tsp salt

Directions

1. In a pan, add the rice and water and bring to a boil.
2. Reduce the heat to medium-low and simmer, covered for about 20-25 minutes.
3. Meanwhile in another large pan, mix together the coconut milk and peanut butter on medium-high heat and cook for about 5-7 minutes.
4. Stir in the chickpeas, ginger, cinnamon and cayenne pepper and cook for about 10 minutes, stirring occasionally.
5. Add the tomatoes and cook for about 10 minutes.
6. Stir in the salt and remove from the heat.
7. Serve the curry over the rice.

OKRA
from Afghanistan

Prep Time: 10 mins
Total Time: 45 mins

Servings per Recipe: 4
Calories   127 kcal
Fat   7.1 g
Carbohydrates 15.2 g
Protein   3.3 g
Cholesterol   0 mg
Sodium   176 mg

Ingredients

2 tbsp vegetable oil
1 onion, thinly sliced
2 tbsp tomato paste
1 lb. okra, sliced in 1/4 inch pieces
1 tsp ground turmeric
salt and black pepper to taste
2 C. water

Directions

1. In a large skillet, heat the oil on medium-low heat and cook the onion for about 15 minutes, stirring occasionally.
2. Add the tomato paste and cook, stirring continuously till no lumps remain.
3. Add the okra, turmeric, salt, pepper and water and bring to a boil on high heat.
4. Reduce the heat to medium-low and simmer for about 15-20 minutes.
5. Season to taste with the salt and pepper if required.

North Indian Inspired Curried Okra

Prep Time: 5 mins
Total Time: 15 mins

Servings per Recipe: 4
Calories	69 kcal
Fat	3.7 g
Carbohydrates	8.5g
Protein	2.4 g
Cholesterol	0 mg
Sodium	301 mg

Ingredients

- 1 lb. okra, ends trimmed, cut into 1/4-inch rounds
- 1 tbsp olive oil
- 1 tsp whole cumin seeds
- 1/2 tsp curry powder
- 1/2 tsp chickpea flour
- 1/2 tsp salt

Directions

1. In a microwave safe plate, place the okra and microwave on High for about 3 minutes.
2. In a large skillet, heat the oil on medium heat and sauté the cumin till it turns golden brown.
3. Stir in the okra and cook for about 5 minutes.
4. Gently, stir in the curry powder, chickpea flour and salt and cook for about 2 minutes.
5. Serve immediately.

SUMMER-TIME
Charred Okra

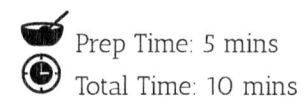

Prep Time: 5 mins
Total Time: 10 mins

Servings per Recipe: 4
Calories   156 kcal
Fat   12 g
Carbohydrates   11.4g
Protein   3 g
Cholesterol   31 mg
Sodium   1501 mg

Ingredients

1 lb. fresh okra
1/4 C. melted butter
1/4 C. Cajun seasoning

Directions

1. Set your grill for high heat and lightly, grease the grill grate.
2. Coat the okra with the melted butter and then roll in the Cajun seasoning.
3. Cook the okra on the grill for about 2 minutes per side.

Barbados Style Okra

Prep Time: 10 mins
Total Time: 25 mins

Servings per Recipe: 6
Calories	96 kcal
Fat	6.9 g
Carbohydrates	8.6g
Protein	1.8 g
Cholesterol	0 mg
Sodium	7 mg

Ingredients

3 tbsp olive oil
1 large onion, thinly sliced
2 cloves garlic, minced
4 C. fresh okra, ends trimmed and halved lengthwise
salt to taste
ground black pepper to taste
1 lime, juiced

Directions

1. In a large skillet, heat the oil on medium heat and sauté the onion and garlic for about 5 minutes.
2. Stir in the okra, salt and pepper and increase the heat to high.
3. Cook, stirring occasionally for about 10 minutes.
4. Stir in the lime juice and cook for about 2 minutes.

LOUISIANA
Okra

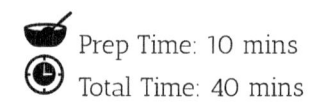

Prep Time: 10 mins
Total Time: 40 mins

Servings per Recipe: 4
Calories	133 kcal
Fat	7.2 g
Carbohydrates	14.2g
Protein	4 g
Cholesterol	0 mg
Sodium	184 mg

Ingredients

2 tbsp olive oil
1/2 large onion, chopped
2 cloves garlic, minced
1/2 green bell pepper, chopped
1 (16 oz.) can diced tomatoes in juice
3/8 tsp dried thyme

2 tbsp chopped fresh parsley
1/4 tsp cayenne pepper
salt and pepper to taste
1 (16 oz.) package frozen cut okra

Directions

1. In a large skillet, heat the oil on medium heat and sauté the onion and garlic till tender.
2. Add the green pepper and cook and till tender.
3. Drain the tomatoes, reserving juice.
4. Stir in the skillet, add the tomatoes, thyme, parsley, cayenne, salt and pepper.
5. Simmer for about 5 minutes on medium heat.
6. Add the frozen okra and add the enough reserved juice of tomatoes to cover the bottom of the pan.
7. Cook, covered for about 15 minutes.

Andhra Style Okra Stir-Fry

Prep Time: 10 mins
Total Time: 25 mins

Servings per Recipe: 2
Calories	262 kcal
Fat	21.1 g
Carbohydrates	18g
Protein	5.1 g
Cholesterol	0 mg
Sodium	45 mg

Ingredients

- 1 lb. fresh okra
- salt to taste
- 2 tsp chili powder
- 3 tbsp olive oil
- 1 pinch asafoetida powder
- 1/2 tsp brown mustard seeds

Directions

1. Rinse the okra and cut head and tail end off of each okra.
2. Chop the okra into small pieces.
3. In a small bowl, mix together the okra, salt, chili powder and asafoetida powder.
4. In a medium skillet, heat the oil on medium-high heat oil and sauté the black mustard seeds till they pop.
5. Add the okra mixture into the skillet and cook, covered for about 10-15 minutes.
6. Serve hot.

SOUTHERN
Okra and Grits Fritters

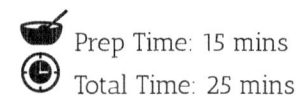

Prep Time: 15 mins
Total Time: 25 mins

Servings per Recipe: 6
Calories	196 kcal
Fat	4 g
Carbohydrates	35.7g
Protein	8 g
Cholesterol	62 mg
Sodium	343 mg

Ingredients

2 lb. fresh okra, sliced in 1/8 inch pieces
1 large tomato, diced
1 onion, diced
6 packets instant grits
2 eggs, lightly beaten
salt and black pepper to taste
1/2 C. oil for frying

Directions

1. In a large bowl, mix together the okra, tomato and onion.
2. Add the grits, eggs, salt and pepper and with your hands, mix till well combined.
3. Make about 2 1/2-inch sized patties from the mixture.
4. In a cast iron skillet, heat the oil on medium-high heat.
5. Add the fritter and cook for about 5 minutes per side.
6. Transfer the patties onto the paper towel lined plate to drain.
7. Serve immediately.

South Carolina Inspired Deep Fried Okra

Prep Time: 15 mins
Total Time: 30 mins

Servings per Recipe: 4
Calories	394 kcal
Fat	29.2 g
Carbohydrates	29 g
Protein	4.7 g
Cholesterol	46 mg
Sodium	167 mg

Ingredients

- 10 pods okra, sliced in 1/4 inch pieces
- 1 egg, beaten
- 1 C. cornmeal
- 1/4 tsp salt
- 1/4 tsp ground black pepper
- 1/2 C. vegetable oil

Directions

1. In a small bowl, soak the okra in egg for about 5-10 minutes.
2. In a bowl, mix together the cornmeal, salt and pepper.
3. In a large skillet, heat the oil on medium-high heat.
4. Coat the okra with the cornmeal mixture evenly.
5. Stir in the okra in hot oil and stir continuously.
6. Reduce the heat to medium when okra first starts to brown and cook till golden.
7. Transfer the okra onto the paper towel lined plate to drain.

OKRA
Burgers

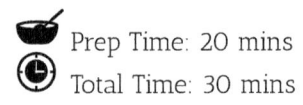

🥣 Prep Time: 20 mins
🕐 Total Time: 30 mins

Servings per Recipe: 6
Calories   224 kcal
Fat   12.3 g
Carbohydrates   25.1g
Protein   4.8 g
Cholesterol   31 mg
Sodium   467 mg

Ingredients

3 C. vegetable oil for frying
1 lb. okra, finely chopped
1 C. finely chopped onion
1 tsp salt
1/4 tsp pepper
1/2 C. water

1 egg
1/2 C. all-purpose flour
1 tsp baking powder
1/2 C. cornmeal

Directions

1. In a large skillet, heat 1-inch of the oil to 375 degrees F.
2. In a bowl, mix together the flour, baking powder and cornmeal.
3. In a large bowl, mix together the okra, onion, salt, pepper, water and egg.
4. Add the flour mixture into the okra mixture and stir to combine.
5. Carefully, place the okra mixture by spoonfuls into the hot oil and fry for about 2 minutes per side.
6. With a slotted spoon, transfer onto the paper towel lined plate to drain.

Baton Rouge Vegetarian Gumbo

Prep Time: 15 mins
Total Time: 1 hr 15 mins

Servings per Recipe: 8
Calories	105 kcal
Fat	5.5 g
Carbohydrates	12.4g
Protein	3.2 g
Cholesterol	0 mg
Sodium	542 mg

Ingredients

- 1 tbsp vegetable oil
- 1 clove garlic, minced
- 1 medium onion, finely chopped
- 1 medium green bell pepper, finely chopped
- 1/2 (16 oz.) package frozen okra, thawed and sliced
- 8 oz. fresh mushrooms, sliced
- 1 (14.5 oz.) can diced tomatoes with juice
- 1 (6 oz.) can tomato paste
- 1/2 tsp file powder
- 2 bay leaves
- 1 tsp salt
- 1 tsp ground black pepper
- 2 tbsp vegetable oil
- 2 tbsp all-purpose flour

Directions

1. In a large pan, heat 1 tbsp of the oil on medium heat and sauté the garlic, onion and green bell pepper till tender.
2. Stir in the okra, mushrooms, and diced tomatoes with liquid, tomato paste, file powder, bay leaves, salt and pepper.
3. Cook for about 40 minutes, stirring occasionally.
4. In a medium skillet, heat 2 tbsp of the oil on medium heat.
5. Slowly, add the flour, stirring continuously and cook till a golden brown roux is formed.
6. Place the roux into the okra mixture and cook, stirring occasionally for about 5-10 minutes.

SPRING
Veggies Fiesta

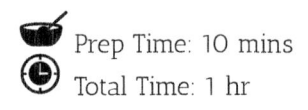

Prep Time: 10 mins
Total Time: 1 hr

Servings per Recipe: 4
Calories   193 kcal
Fat   14.1 g
Carbohydrates   15.8g
Protein   4.3 g
Cholesterol   0 mg
Sodium   9 mg

Ingredients

1 eggplant, quartered and cut into 1/2-inch pieces
2 small yellow squash, halved lengthwise and sliced
1 bunch fresh asparagus, cut into 2-inch pieces
1 red bell pepper, seeded and cut into strips
1/2 red onion, sliced

4 cloves garlic
1/4 C. olive oil
1/4 C. red wine vinegar
1/4 C. chopped fresh parsley
2 lemons, juiced
3 tbsp chopped fresh oregano
salt and freshly ground black pepper to taste

Directions

1. Before you do anything set the oven to 400 F. Coat a baking pan with some oil or cooking spray.
2. Lay in it the eggplant, yellow squash, asparagus, red bell pepper, red onion, and garlic. Cook them in the oven for 17 min.
3. Get a small bowl: Whisk in it the olive oil, vinegar, parsley, lemon juice, oregano, salt, and pepper to make the vinaigrette.
4. Drizzle the vinaigrette over the veggies then serve it.
5. Enjoy.

Zesty Veggies Roast

Prep Time: 45 mins
Total Time: 2 hrs 15 mins

Servings per Recipe: 8
Calories	297 kcal
Fat	4.2 g
Carbohydrates	64.7g
Protein	6 g
Cholesterol	0 mg
Sodium	103 mg

Ingredients

- 1 large butternut squash - peeled, seeded, and cut into 1-inch pieces
- 1 large delicata squash - peeled, seeded, and cut into 1-inch pieces
- 3 sweet potatoes, peeled and cut into 1-inch pieces
- 1 (2 lb) rutabaga, peeled and cut into 1-inch pieces
- 2 red potatoes, peeled and cut into 1-inch pieces
- 2 carrots, sliced
- 1 large onion, sliced
- 2 tbsp dried rosemary
- 2 tbsp dried thyme
- 1 tsp dried oregano
- 2 tbsp extra-virgin olive oil
- 6 dried bay leaves
- 1 dash lemon juice
- 1 dash red wine vinegar
- 1 pinch salt
- 1 pinch ground black pepper

Directions

1. Before you do anything set the oven to 400 F. Coat a roasting dish with some oil or cooking spray.
2. Get a large bowl: Toss the butternut squash, delicata squash, sweet potato, rutabaga, and red potato pieces, carrots, and onion.
3. Get a small bowl: Stir in it the thyme with oregano and rosemary. Toss the veggies with the herbs mix and olive oil. Spread the veggies in the roasting dish.
4. Top them with vinegar, lemon juice and bay leaves, a pinch of salt and pepper. Cook the veggies in the oven for 1 h 32 min while stirring them 3 time. Serve your veggies warm.
5. Enjoy.

CHERRY Potato Roast Salad

Prep Time: 15 mins
Total Time: 1 hr 30 mins

Servings per Recipe: 6
Calories   289 kcal
Fat   9.1 g
Carbohydrates   47.3g
Protein   8.6 g
Cholesterol   0 mg
Sodium   58 mg

Ingredients

- 12 new potatoes, halved
- 2 large red onions, each cut into 8 wedges
- 2 large yellow bell peppers, seeded and cubed
- 4 cloves garlic, peeled
- 1 eggplant, thickly sliced (optional)
- 1 tsp chopped fresh rosemary
- 2 tsps chopped fresh thyme
- 2 tbsp olive oil
- salt to taste
- 1 pint cherry tomatoes, halved
- 1/3 C. toasted pine nuts
- 1 (10 oz) bag baby spinach leaves
- 2 tbsp balsamic vinegar

Directions

1. Before you do anything set the oven to 400 F. Cover a baking pan with a large piece of foil.
2. Lay the potato in a ovenproof plate and microwave it for 5 min until it becomes soft.
3. Get a large bowl: Toss the cooked potato with onion, bell pepper, garlic, and eggplant, rosemary, thyme, and olive oil, a pinch of salt and pepper.
4. Transfer the veggies mix to the baking pan. Cook them in the oven for 37 min. Add the cherry tomatoes and cook them for 17 min.
5. Get a large bowl: Add the roasted veggies with spinach, vinegar and pine nuts. Stir them well and serve them.
6. Enjoy.

Rosemary Roasted Rooty Veggies

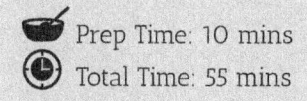

Prep Time: 10 mins
Total Time: 55 mins

Servings per Recipe: 14
Calories	135 kcal
Fat	2.6 g
Carbohydrates	27.4g
Protein	2.8 g
Cholesterol	0 mg
Sodium	116 mg

Ingredients

- parsnips, peeled
- 6 large carrots, peeled
- 1 celery root, peeled
- 1 rutabaga, peeled
- 1 yellow onion, peeled
- 3 tbsp minced garlic
- 3 tbsp dried rosemary
- 2 tbsp extra-virgin olive oil
- sea salt and freshly ground black pepper to taste

Directions

1. Before you do anything set the oven to 400 F.
2. Finely chop the veggies into 1 inch pieces. Transfer them to a large zip lock bag with garlic, rosemary, olive oil, salt, and pepper.
3. Shake the bag to coat the veggies with herbs. Spread them on a lined up baking pan. Cook them in the oven for 47 min. Serve your roasted veggies warm.
4. Enjoy.

BABY
Herbed Veggies Roast

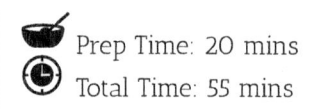

Prep Time: 20 mins
Total Time: 55 mins

Servings per Recipe: 7
Calories   171 kcal
Fat   8 g
Carbohydrates   23.4g
Protein   2.9 g
Cholesterol   0 mg
Sodium   16 mg

Ingredients

- 1 1/2 lb new potatoes, quartered
- 1/2 C. baby carrots
- 1 small onion, cut into wedges
- 1/4 C. olive oil
- 3 tbsp lemon juice
- 3 cloves garlic, minced
- 1 tbsp chopped fresh rosemary
- 1 tbsp dried oregano
- salt and pepper to taste
- 1/2 small eggplant, quartered and cut into 1/2-inch st
- 1 red bell pepper, cut into 1/2-inch wide strips

Directions

1. Before you do anything set the oven to 450 F.
2. Place the onion with carrot and potato in a casserole dish. Get a mixing bowl: Add the olive oil, lemon juice, garlic, rosemary, oregano, salt and pepper. Mix them well.
3. Drizzle the mix all over the veggies and toss them. Cook them in the oven for 22 min. Add the bell pepper with eggplant and stir them.
4. Roast the veggies again for 17 min. Serve your roast hot.
5. Enjoy.

Crunchy Roasted Veggies Pie

Prep Time: 20 mins
Total Time: 20 mins

Servings per Recipe: 4
Calories	619 kcal
Fat	42.9 g
Carbohydrates	41.1g
Protein	17.1 g
Cholesterol	67 mg
Sodium	1156 mg

Ingredients

- 1 onion, chopped
- 1 green bell pepper, chopped
- 1 red bell pepper, chopped
- 1 green chile pepper, chopped
- 1 clove garlic, chopped
- freshly ground black pepper to taste
- 1 tbsp extra virgin olive oil
- 1 (14.5 oz) can diced tomatoes, drained
- 1 (4 oz) package feta cheese, crumbled
- 1/2 (17.5 oz) package frozen puff pastry (1 sheet), thawed

Directions

1. Before you do anything set the oven to 450 F. Grease a cake or pie pan.
2. Toss the peppers with garlic, onion, a drizzle of olive oil, a pinch of salt and pepper in the pie pan. Stir them and cook them in the oven for 12 min.
3. Lay the tomato over the layer of veggies and lay on it the cheese followed by the puff pastry. Place the pie in the oven and cook it for 22 min.
4. Flip the pie and serve it hot right away.
5. Enjoy.

EGG
Salad

🥣 Prep Time: 10 mins
🕐 Total Time: 35 mins

Servings per Recipe: 4
Calories   344 kcal
Fat   31.9 g
Carbohydrates   2.3g
Protein   < 13 g
Cholesterol   382 mg
Sodium   1351 mg

Ingredients

8 eggs
1/2 C. mayonnaise
1 tsp prepared yellow mustard
1/4 C. diced green onion
salt and pepper to taste
1/4 tsp paprika

Directions

1. Boil your eggs in water for 2 mins then place a lid on the pot and let the contents sit for 15 mins. Once the eggs have cooled remove their shells and dice them.
2. Now get a bowl, combine: green onions, eggs, mustard, and mayo.
3. Stir the mix until it is smooth then add in the paprika, pepper, and salt.
4. Stir the contents again then enjoy with toasted buns.

Amish Pasta Salad

Prep Time: 15 mins
Total Time: 1 hr 25 mins

Servings per Recipe: 6
Calories	532 kcal
Fat	25.3 g
Carbohydrates	66g
Protein	9 g
Cholesterol	133 mg
Sodium	944 mg

Ingredients

- 2 C. uncooked elbow macaroni
- 3 hard-cooked eggs, diced
- 1 small onion, diced
- 3 stalks celery, diced
- 1 small red bell pepper, seeded and diced
- 2 tbsps dill pickle relish
- 2 C. creamy salad dressing (e.g. Miracle Whip)
- 3 tbsps prepared yellow mustard
- 3/4 C. white sugar
- 2 1/4 tsps white vinegar
- 1/4 tsp salt
- 3/4 tsp celery seed

Directions

1. Boil your pasta in water and salt for 9 mins. Then remove the liquids.
2. Get a bowl combine: relish, eggs, red pepper, onions, and celery.
3. Get a 2nd bowl, combine: celery seeds, dressing, salt, mustard, vinegar, and white sugar.
4. Combine both bowls then add the pasta and stir everything again.
5. Place a covering of plastic around the bowl and put everything in the fridge for 65 mins.
6. Enjoy.

ELEGANT
Cucumber Salad

Prep Time: 10 mins
Total Time: 10 mins

Servings per Recipe: 8
Calories   99 kcal
Fat   0.2 g
Carbohydrates   24.9 g
Protein   1.1 g
Cholesterol   0 mg
Sodium   4 mg

Ingredients

4 cucumbers, thinly sliced
1 small white onion, thinly sliced
1 C. white vinegar
1/2 C. water

3/4 C. white sugar
1 tbsp dried dill, or to taste

Directions

1. Get a bowl, combine: onions and cucumbers.
2. Now get the following boiling: sugar, water, and vinegar.
3. Once the mix is boiling combine it with the onions and cucumbers.
4. Stir the contents then add the dill and stir everything again.
5. Place a covering of plastic around the bowl and put everything in the fridge until it all is chilled.
6. Enjoy.

Cashew Salad

Prep Time: 15 mins
Total Time: 15 mins

Servings per Recipe: 6
Calories	133 kcal
Fat	8 g
Carbohydrates	14.9 g
Protein	2.9 g
Cholesterol	0 mg
Sodium	176 mg

Ingredients

- 1 mango - peeled, seeded and cubed
- 1 Granny Smith apple - peeled, cored and diced
- 3/4 C. toasted cashews
- 1 tbsp balsamic vinegar
- 1/2 tsp ground cinnamon
- 1/4 tsp ground ginger
- 1 pinch salt

Directions

1. Get a bowl, combine: salt, mango, ginger, apples, cinnamon, cashews, and balsamic.
2. Place a covering of plastic around the bowl and put everything in the fridge until it is chilled.
3. Enjoy.

ALMOND
Salad I

🍲 Prep Time: 10 mins
🕒 Total Time: 1 hr 10 mins

Servings per Recipe: 4
Calories   491 kcal
Fat   35.2 g
Carbohydrates   42.9 g
Protein   6 g
Cholesterol   0 mg
Sodium   63 mg

Ingredients

2 tbsps sesame seeds
1 tbsp poppy seeds
1/2 C. white sugar
1/2 C. olive oil
1/4 C. distilled white vinegar
1/4 tsp paprika
1/4 tsp Worcestershire sauce

1 tbsp minced onion
10 oz. fresh spinach - rinsed, dried and torn into bite-size pieces
1 quart strawberries - cleaned, hulled and sliced
1/4 C. almonds, blanched and slivered

Directions

1. Get a bowl, combine: onions, sesame seeds, Worcestershire, poppy seeds, paprika, vinegar, sugar, and olive oil.
2. Place a covering of plastic around the bowl and put the mix in the fridge for 65 mins.
3. Get a 2nd bowl, combine: almonds, spinach, and strawberries.
4. Toss the mix then add the wet mix and toss the contents again.
5. Place the salad in the fridge for 20 mins.
6. Enjoy.

Maggie's Favorite Easy Rigatoni

Prep Time: 15 mins
Total Time: 55 mins

Servings per Recipe: 8
Calories   295 kcal
Carbohydrates   48.8 g
Cholesterol   0 mg
Fat   8.3 g
Protein   8.9 g
Sodium   145 mg

Ingredients

- 1/4 C. olive oil
- 2 cloves garlic, diced
- 1 eggplant, peeled and cut into 1/2-inch cubes
- 1 (28 oz) can plum tomatoes with juice, chopped
- 1 (16 oz) package rigatoni pasta

Directions

1. Boil your rigatoni in salt and water for 12 mins until al dente. Remove excess liquid and set aside.
2. Get a frying pan: stir fry your garlic for 3 mins in olive oil. Add in your eggplants and fry for another 6 mins. Combine in your tomatoes and juice and simmer for 22 mins.
3. Cover pasta with eggplants and sauce.
4. Enjoy.

CANNELLINI
Classic

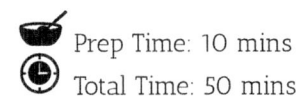

Prep Time: 10 mins
Total Time: 50 mins

Servings per Recipe: 4
Calories   452 kcal
Carbohydrates   59.3 g
Cholesterol   16 mg
Fat   17.7 g
Protein   15.7 g
Sodium   228 mg

Ingredients

3 cloves garlic, diced
1 onion, chopped
1 carrot, finely chopped
2 tbsps chopped fresh parsley
2 tsps dried basil
1 tsp dried oregano
4 tbsps olive oil
1 (14.5 oz) can whole peeled tomatoes
2 C. cooked cannellini beans, drained and rinsed
8 oz macaroni
2 tbsps butter
1/4 C. grated Parmesan cheese
salt and pepper to taste

Directions

1. Stir fry, in olive oil, until onions are soft: onions, basil, carrots, garlic, parsley, and oregano. Mix in some salt and pepper, tomatoes, and 1/4 C. of tomato juice. Cook for 12 mins.
2. Combine in the cannellini and place a lid on the pan. Simmer for 20 mins with lower heat.
3. Boil your macaroni in salt and water until al dente about 10 to 12 mins. Then coat with butter and parmesan. Mix the coated noodles with the cannellini and enjoy.
4. Servings: 4 to 6 servings

Pasta Rustic

Prep Time: 10 mins
Total Time: 35 mins

Servings per Recipe: 4
Calories	717 kcal
Carbohydrates	92.8 g
Cholesterol	31 mg
Fat	32.9 g
Protein	18.1 g
Sodium	491 mg

Ingredients

- 1 lb farfalle (bow tie) pasta
- 1/3 C. olive oil
- 1 clove garlic, chopped
- 1/4 C. butter
- 2 small zucchini, quartered and sliced
- 1 onion, chopped
- 1 tomato, chopped
- 1 (8 oz) package mushrooms, sliced
- 1 tbsp dried oregano
- 1 tbsp paprika
- salt and pepper to taste

Directions

1. Boil your pasta for 10 mins in water and salt. Remove excess liquid and set aside.
2. Fry your salt, pepper, garlic, paprika, zucchini, oregano, mushrooms, onion, and tomato, for 17 mins in olive oil.
3. Mix the veggies and pasta.
4. Enjoy.

SIMPLE
Sundried Tomato Pasta

Prep Time: 8 hrs
Total Time: 8 hrs 20 mins

Servings per Recipe: 6
Calories	1027 kcal
Carbohydrates	102.5 g
Cholesterol	19 mg
Fat	59.4 g
Protein	24.5 g
Sodium	857 mg

Ingredients

2/3 C. chopped fresh basil
1 (28 oz) can diced tomatoes
1 1/2 tsps diced garlic
1 (6 oz) can sliced black olives
1 1/2 C. olive oil
1 tsp salt
1 tsp ground black pepper
1/2 C. chopped fresh chives

1/2 C. chopped sun-dried tomatoes
1 tsp mashed red pepper flakes
6 oz goat cheese
2 (16 oz) packages farfalle pasta

Directions

1. Get a bowl, mix: pepper flakes, basil, sun dried tomatoes, diced tomatoes, chives, garlic, pepper, olives, salt, and olive oil. Place plastic over the bowl, and set in the fridge for 7 to 12 hours.
2. Before using the mix, let it get to room temp.
3. Boil your pasta in salt and water for 10 mins. Remove the excess liquid, mix pasta with sauce, and goat cheese.
4. Enjoy.

A Light Thai Inspired Pasta

Prep Time: 10 mins
Total Time: 15 mins

Servings per Recipe: 4
Calories	254 kcal
Carbohydrates	43.4 g
Cholesterol	0 mg
Fat	5.9 g
Protein	8.7 g
Sodium	43 mg

Ingredients

- 1 tbsp sesame oil
- 8 oz dry fettuccine pasta
- 1/2 tsp soy sauce
- 2 green onions, chopped
- 3/4 C. fresh bean sprouts
- 1 pinch cayenne pepper
- 1 pinch ground white pepper
- 1 pinch garlic powder
- 1 tbsp toasted sesame seeds

Directions

1. Boil your pasta for 10 mins in salt and water. Drain excess liquid. Set aside.
2. Get a frying pan, stir fry: pasta, soy sauce, garlic powder, green onions, pepper, bean sprouts, black pepper, and cayenne for 5 mins.
3. Garnish with toasted sesame.
4. Enjoy.

EASY
Mushroom Pasta

Prep Time: 3 mins
Total Time: 15 mins

Servings per Recipe: 5
Calories   526 kcal
Carbohydrates   64.2 g
Cholesterol   106 mg
Fat   22
Protein   18.2 g
Sodium   889 mg

Ingredients

2/3 C. chopped fresh basil
1 (16 oz) package egg noodles
1 (10.75 oz) can condensed cream of mushroom soup
1 C. cubed processed cheese
2 tbsps butter

1/4 C. milk
1 tsp garlic powder
salt and pepper to taste

Directions

1. Boil your pasta in salt and water for 10 mins. Remove excess liquid.
2. Get a pan and heat and stir until cheese melted: salt and pepper, mushroom soup, garlic powder, cheese, milk, and butter.
3. Once your cheese is melted mix in your noodles and heat for 1 more min. Coat evenly.
4. Enjoy.

Garden Lasagna III (Broccoli, Carrots, & Corn)

Prep Time: 30 mins
Total Time: 1 hr 10 mins

Servings per Recipe: 8
Calories   534 kcal
Carbohydrates   48.8 g
Cholesterol   103 mg
Fat   27 g
Protein   26.6 g
Sodium   1091 mg

Ingredients

- 1 box lasagna noodles
- 2 eggs, beaten
- 1 box part-skim ricotta cheese
- 2 cans condensed cream of mushroom soup
- 2 C. shredded Cheddar cheese
- 1 C. grated Parmesan cheese
- 1 C. sour cream
- 1 package herb and garlic soup mix
- 1 bag chopped frozen broccoli, thawed
- 1 bag frozen sliced carrots
- 1 bag frozen corn kernels

Directions

1. Set your oven to 375 degrees before anything else.
2. Boil noodles in water with salt for 10 mins. Remove all water, set aside.
3. Get a bowl, mix: soup mix, beaten eggs, sour cream, ricotta, parmesan, cheddar, and mushroom soup.
4. In your baking layer everything in the following manner: lasagna, cheese mix, carrots, corn, broccoli. Continue until all ingredients used. Cheese should be upmost layer.
5. Cook for 30, with a cover of foil. 10 mins without.
6. Enjoy.

GARBANZOS
and Basil Tofu

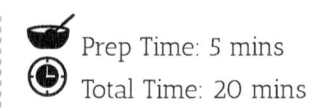

Prep Time: 5 mins
Total Time: 20 mins

Servings per Recipe: 4
Calories   346 kcal
Fat   12.3 g
Carbohydrates   44.7g
Protein   21.7 g
Cholesterol   0 mg
Sodium   849 mg

Ingredients

1 tbsp vegetable oil
1 onion, chopped
1 (14.75 oz.) can creamed corn
1 tbsp curry paste, see appendix
salt to taste
ground black pepper to taste
1/2 tsp garlic powder, or to taste
1 (15 oz.) can garbanzo beans (chickpeas), drained and rinsed
1 (12 oz.) package firm tofu, cubed
1 bunch fresh spinach, stems removed
1 tsp dried basil or to taste

Directions

1. Stir fry your onions until see-through and then add in: curry paste and cream corn.
2. Stir fry the mix for 7 more mins then add: spinach, garlic, tofu, pepper, garbanzos, and salt.
3. Place a lid on the pot and cook everything for 3 more mins before shutting the heat and adding in the basil.
4. Enjoy.

Easy BBQ Tofu

Prep Time: 10 mins
Total Time: 8 hrs 35 mins

Servings per Recipe: 4
Calories   409 kcal
Fat   17.2 g
Carbohydrates   50.4 g
Protein   15.2 g
Cholesterol   0 mg
Sodium   1348 mg

Ingredients

1 (16 oz.) package extra firm tofu, pressed, and cut into strips
3 tbsps olive oil
1 egg white
1 tbsp barbeque sauce
1 C. all-purpose flour
1 tsp salt
1/2 tsp pepper
1 C. barbeque sauce

Directions

1. Freeze your sliced tofu throughout the night. Then thaw out the tofu and dry the pieces.
2. Get a bowl, combine: 1 tbsp bbq sauce, and egg whites.
3. Get a 2nd bowl, combine: pepper, flour, and salt.
4. Get your olive oil hot, and turn on your broiler before doing anything else.
5. Now coat your tofu with the egg and dry mix.
6. Fry the pieces for 60 secs per side.
7. Layer the tofu pieces in a broiler pan or dish and top everything with the rest of the bbq sauce.
8. Cook the tofu pieces under the broiler for 6 mins per side.
9. Enjoy with some more bbq sauce.

EASY
BBQ Tofu II

Prep Time: 5 mins
Total Time: 15 mins

Servings per Recipe: 6
Calories	336 kcal
Fat	12.5 g
Carbohydrates	47.1g
Protein	9.4 g
Cholesterol	0 mg
Sodium	945 mg

Ingredients

1 (12 oz.) package extra firm tofu, pressed and drained, cut into 1/4 inch slices.
3 tbsps vegetable oil

1 onion, thinly sliced
1 1/2 C. barbecue sauce
6 hamburger buns

Directions

1. Brown both sides of your tofu slices in veggie oil then add the onions and continue browning for about 7 more mins until the onions are soft.
2. Add in the bbq sauce and cook the mix for 7 more mins with a low level of heat.
3. Serve the tofu pieces on sesame seed buns.
4. Enjoy.

Orange Chili Carrot Tofu

Prep Time: 15 mins
Total Time: 30 mins

Servings per Recipe: 4
Calories   286 kcal
Fat   15 g
Carbohydrates   23.3g
Protein   18.9 g
Cholesterol   0 mg
Sodium   500 mg

Ingredients

- 1/4 C. vegetable oil for frying
- 1/4 C. cornstarch
- 1 (16 oz.) package firm tofu, drained and cut into strips
- 2 tbsps soy sauce
- 1/2 C. orange juice
- 1/4 C. warm water
- 1 tbsp sugar
- 1 tsp chili paste
- 1 tsp cornstarch
- 1 tbsp vegetable oil
- 2 carrots, sliced

Directions

1. Get a bowl, combine: cornstarch (1 tsp), soy sauce, chili paste, orange juice, sugar, and water.
2. Coat your tofu with 1/4 a C. of cornstarch then stir fry them in 1/4 a C. of oil for 7 mins, flipping half way.
3. Now set everything to the side on some paper towels.
4. Add in the rest of the oil and fry the carrots until they become soft.
5. Add in the orange juice mix and get it all boiling.
6. Once the contents are boiling add in the tofu and cook everything for 2 more mins before coating the pieces evenly.
7. Enjoy.

RUSTIC
Tofu

🍲 Prep Time: 15 mins
🕐 Total Time: 30 mins

Servings per Recipe: 4
Calories   285 kcal
Fat   17.5 g
Carbohydrates   18.9 g
Protein   16.3 g
Cholesterol   0 mg
Sodium   823 mg

Ingredients

1 (16 oz.) package extra-firm tofu, drained and pressed, cut into 1/2 inch slices, then cut again into 4 cubes
2 C. vegetable broth
3 tbsps vegetable oil
1/2 C. all-purpose flour
3 tbsps nutritional yeast
1 tsp salt
1/2 tsp freshly ground black pepper
1 tsp sage
1/2 tsp cayenne pepper

Directions

1. Cover your tofu with broth in a bowl then let them sit submerged.
2. Get a 2nd bowl, combine: cayenne, flour, sage, yeast, pepper, and salt.
3. Dip your tofu pieces into the dry mix then fry them in hot oil until browned all over.
4. Enjoy.

Cheddar Tofu Quiche I

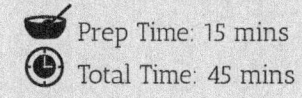

Prep Time: 15 mins
Total Time: 45 mins

Servings per Recipe: 6
Calories   288 kcal
Fat   18.8 g
Carbohydrates   18.5g
Protein   12.7 g
Cholesterol   22 mg
Sodium   489 mg

Ingredients

- 1 (8 oz.) container tofu
- 1/3 C. 1% milk
- 1/2 tsp salt, or to taste
- 1/2 tsp pepper
- 1 (10 oz.) package frozen chopped spinach, thawed and drained
- 1 tsp minced garlic
- 1/4 C. diced onion
- 2/3 C. shredded Cheddar cheese
- 1/2 C. shredded Swiss cheese
- 1 unbaked 9 inch pie crust

Directions

1. Set your oven to 350 degrees before doing anything else.
2. Puree the following in a blender: milk, pepper, salt, and tofu.
3. Get a bowl, mix: tofu puree, spinach, Swiss, garlic, cheddar, and onions.
4. Fill your crust with the mix and cook the contents in the oven for 35 mins.
5. Enjoy.

CELERY
Tofu Salad

🍳 Prep Time: 10 mins
🕐 Total Time: 4 hrs 10 mins

Servings per Recipe: 4
Calories   227 kcal
Fat   15.5 g
Carbohydrates   8.2g
Protein   18.2 g
Cholesterol   3 mg
Sodium   90 mg

Ingredients

1 (16 oz.) package extra-firm tofu, drain 2 tbsps mayonnaise
1 tbsp sweet pickle relish
1 tsp distilled white vinegar
1 tsp prepared mustard
1 tsp white sugar
1/2 tsp ground turmeric
1/4 tsp dried dill weed
1 tbsp dried parsley

1 lb firm tofu, sliced and well drained
1 tbsp minced onion
2 tbsps minced celery
salt to taste
ground black pepper to taste

Directions

1. Get a bowl, mix: parsley, mayo, dill, relish, turmeric, vinegar, sugar, and mustard.
2. Get a 2nd bowl, mashed together: celery, tofu, pepper, salt, and onions.
3. Combine both bowls and add in some extra pepper and salt.
4. Now place everything in the fridge until cold.
5. Enjoy.

Creamy Asiago Tofu

Prep Time: 20 mins
Total Time: 30 mins

Servings per Recipe: 8
Calories   152 kcal
Fat   9.5 g
Carbohydrates   7.3 g
Protein   12.1 g
Cholesterol   16 mg
Sodium   301 mg

Ingredients

1 tbsp butter
1 tbsp olive oil
1 small onion, chopped
2 cloves garlic, minced
2 lbs fresh spinach, washed and chopped
1 (12 oz.) package firm tofu
1/2 C. milk or soy milk

1 C. Asiago cheese
garlic powder to taste
salt and pepper to taste

Directions

1. Puree the following in a blender: pepper, tofu, salt, cheese, and garlic.
2. Stir fry your garlic and onions in olive oil and butter for about 5 mins until see-through.
3. Now combine in the spinach for 3 more mins until tender and then add the puree.
4. Cook the contents until hot for about 3 more mins.
5. Top with asiago.
6. Enjoy.

MEXICAN STYLE
Tofu

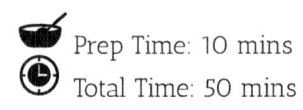

Prep Time: 10 mins
Total Time: 50 mins

Servings per Recipe: 8
Calories   278 kcal
Fat   18.3 g
Carbohydrates   20.2g
Protein   11 g
Cholesterol   15 mg
Sodium   382 mg

Ingredients

1 (16 oz.) package garden herb tofu, crumbled
2 tbsps vegetable oil
1 clove garlic, minced
1/2 C. chopped onion
2 tsps chili powder
1/4 tsp paprika
1/4 tsp cayenne pepper
1/4 tsp ground cumin
1/4 tsp salt
1/2 lime, juiced

1/2 C. tomato sauce
1/4 C. chopped fresh cilantro
10 medium taco shells, heated
2 C. shredded lettuce
2 tomatoes, chopped
1 avocado - peeled, pitted and diced
1 C. shredded Cheddar cheese
1/4 C. salsa

Directions

1. For 7 mins stir fry your onions, garlic, and tofu in oil. Then combine in the tomato sauce, chili powder, lime juice, paprika, salt, cayenne, and cumin.
2. Continue cooking for 5 more mins. Then add the cilantro.
3. Fill your shells with the mix and then layer some salsa, lettuce, cheese, avocadoes, and tomatoes.
4. Enjoy.

Lasagna II
(Vegan Approved)

Prep Time: 30 mins
Total Time: 2 hrs 30 mins

Servings per Recipe: 8
Calories   511 kcal
Fat   15.8 g
Carbohydrates   69.9 g
Protein   32.5 g
Cholesterol   0 mg
Sodium   1074 mg

Ingredients

- 2 tbsps olive oil
- 1 1/2 C. chopped onion
- 3 tbsps minced garlic
- 4 (14.5 oz.) cans stewed tomatoes
- 1/3 C. tomato paste
- 1/2 C. chopped fresh basil
- 1/2 C. chopped parsley
- 1 tsp salt
- 1 tsp ground black pepper
- 1 (16 oz.) package lasagna noodles
- 2 lbs firm tofu
- 2 tbsps minced garlic
- 1/4 C. chopped fresh basil
- 1/4 C. chopped parsley
- 1/2 tsp salt
- ground black pepper to taste
- 3 (10 oz.) packages frozen chopped spinach, thawed and drained

Directions

1. Stir fry your onions in olive oil for 7 mins then add in the garlic and cook for 7 more mins.
2. Now add: parsley, tomatoes, pepper, salt, basil, and tomato paste.
3. Get the mix boiling, then place a lid on the pot, and let the contents gently cook with a low level of heat for 65 mins.
4. Simultaneously boil your noodles in water and salt for 9 mins. Then remove all the liquid.
5. Get a bowl, mash: pepper, tofu, salt, garlic, parsley, and basil.
6. Set your oven to 400 degrees before, doing anything else.
7. Now get a baking dish and layer the following in it: noodles, 1/3 tofu mix, spinach, 1.5 C. sauce, and more noodles.
8. Continue for all of the ingredients and end with some sauce.
9. Cover the dish with foil and cook it all in the oven for 35 mins.
10. Enjoy.

SWEET
Tofu Stir Fry

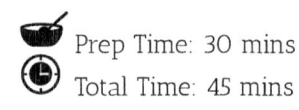

Prep Time: 30 mins
Total Time: 45 mins

Servings per Recipe: 4
Calories   215 kcal
Fat   9.4 g
Carbohydrates   24g
Protein   13.6 g
Cholesterol   0 mg
Sodium   507 mg

Ingredients

1 tbsp vegetable oil
1/2 medium onion, sliced
2 cloves garlic, finely chopped
1 tbsp fresh ginger root, finely chopped
1 (16 oz.) package tofu, drained and cut into cubes
1/2 C. water
4 tbsps rice wine vinegar
2 tbsps honey
2 tbsps soy sauce
2 tsps cornstarch dissolved in
2 tbsps water
1 carrot, peeled and sliced
1 green bell pepper, seeded and cut into strips
1 C. baby corn, drained and cut into pieces
1 small head bok choy, chopped
2 C. fresh mushrooms, chopped
1 1/4 C. bean sprouts
1 C. bamboo shoots, drained and chopped
1/2 tsp crushed red pepper
2 medium green onions, thinly sliced diagonally

Directions

1. Stir fry your onions for 2 mins in oil then add the ginger and garlic.
2. Cook this mix for 1 more min before adding the tofu and frying until it has browned.
3. Now add the corn, carrots, and bell peppers and cook for 4 more mins then add the red pepper, bok choy, bamboo, mushrooms, and bean sprouts.
4. Cook for 1 more min to get everything hot then shut the heat.
5. In a smaller pot and get the following simmering with a high level of heat and then a low one: soy sauce, water, honey, and vinegar.
6. Simmer for 4 mins then add the water and cornstarch mix.
7. Cook the mix until everything becomes a thick sauce.
8. Top your tofu with this sauce.
9. Now add scallions when serving.
10. Enjoy.

American Style Tofu

Prep Time: 5 mins
Total Time: 25 mins

Servings per Recipe: 4
Calories	532 kcal
Fat	20.3 g
Carbohydrates	67.1g
Protein	27 g
Cholesterol	23 mg
Sodium	262 mg

Ingredients

- 3 tbsps butter
- 1 lb firm tofu, sliced into 1/4 inch slices
- 2 C. whole wheat flour
- 1 C. water
- 1/4 C. dry white wine
- 2 cubes vegetable bouillon
- 4 tbsps prepared mustard
- 1/4 C. honey

Directions

1. Coat your tofu with flour and fry them in butter.
2. Get the tofu browned all over and then add in bouillon, water, and wine.
3. Get everything gently boiling and let it go for 12 mins.
4. Now finally add in the honey and mustard.
5. Enjoy.

INDIAN STYLE
Tofu

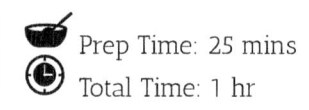

🍲 Prep Time: 25 mins
🕐 Total Time: 1 hr

Servings per Recipe: 6
Calories   413 kcal
Fat   27.8 g
Carbohydrates   33.2g
Protein   15.1 g
Cholesterol   0 mg
Sodium   401 mg

Ingredients

- 3 tbsps vegetable oil
- 2 inch piece fresh ginger root, peeled and minced
- 2 onions, halved and sliced
- 1/2 head cauliflower, cut into florets
- 3 carrots, peeled and sliced
- 3 tbsps vindaloo curry powder
- 6 tbsps tomato paste
- 1 (15 oz.) can coconut milk
- 1 C. vegetable broth
- 1 (15 oz.) can garbanzo beans (chickpeas), drained and rinsed
- 1 lb extra-firm tofu, cut into 1-inch cubes
- 1 C. mushrooms, sliced
- salt to taste

Directions

1. Stir fry your ginger in veggie oil in a big pot for 3 mins then add in: carrots, cauliflower, and onions.
2. Cook the mix for about 7 more mins while stirring.
3. Now add in the tomato paste, and vindaloo.
4. Stir everything evenly and then add: beans, salt, mushrooms, tofu, coconut milk, and broth.
5. Get the mix boiling, and then place a lid on the pot, set the heat to low, and let the contents gently boil for 17 mins.
6. Enjoy.

Cilantro and Sesame Tofu

Prep Time: 25 mins
Total Time: 1 hr 25 mins

Servings per Recipe: 4
Calories	419 kcal
Fat	33.6 g
Carbohydrates	14.6 g
Protein	20 g
Cholesterol	0 mg
Sodium	1224 mg

Ingredients

- 1 lb firm tofu, cut into 4 pieces, then cut diagonally, into 8 triangles, pressed and drained
- 1 C. fresh orange juice
- 1/4 C. rice vinegar
- 1/3 C. soy sauce
- 1/3 C. canola oil
- 4 tsps dark sesame oil
- 3 cloves garlic, minced
- 1 tbsp minced fresh ginger root
- 1/4 tsp red pepper flakes
- 1 green onions, cut into 1-inch strips
- 1/4 C. coarsely chopped fresh cilantro
- 2 dried chipotle chili pepper, stems removed, and diced

Directions

1. Get a bowl, combine: cilantro, pepper flakes, onions, orange juice, ginger, chilies, vinegar, oils, and soy sauce.
2. Layer all your tofu pieces into a casserole dish and top with the orange sauce.
3. Place a covering of plastic around the dish and put everything in the fridge for 40 mins.
4. Set your oven to 350 degrees before doing anything else.
5. Remove about half of the marinade from the dish and cook it all in the oven for 50 mins.
6. Enjoy.

TOFU
Party Dip

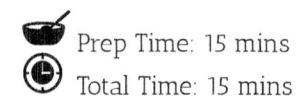

🥣 Prep Time: 15 mins
🕐 Total Time: 15 mins

Servings per Recipe: 4
Calories   370 kcal
Fat   31.8 g
Carbohydrates   7.2g
Protein   18.8 g
Cholesterol   10 mg
Sodium   632 mg

Ingredients

1 lb firm tofu, pressed, drained, and then frozen
1 stalk celery, chopped
1 green onion, chopped
1/2 C. mayonnaise

2 tbsps soy sauce
1 tbsp lemon juice

Directions

1. Take your frozen tofu and thaw it.
2. Once the tofu is no longer frozen press out any liquids.
3. Add the tofu to a bowl and mash it.
4. Combine with the tofu: lemon juice, celery, soy sauce, onions, and mayo.
5. Place the mix in the fridge to chill.
6. Enjoy.

Traditional Indian Curry Paste

Prep Time: 5 mins
Total Time: 5 mins

Servings per Recipe: 4
Calories	225.4
Fat	10.4 g
Cholesterol	0 mg
Sodium	91 mg
Carbohydrates	33.3 g
Protein	8.8 g

Ingredients

- 2 1/2 tbsps coriander seeds, ground
- 1 tbsp cumin seed, ground
- 1 tsp brown mustard seeds
- 1/2 tsp cracked black peppercorns
- 1 tsp chili powder
- 1 tsp ground turmeric
- 2 crushed garlic cloves
- 2 tsps grated fresh ginger
- 3-4 tbsps white vinegar

Directions

1. Get a bowl, combine: coriander seeds, cumin seeds, mustard seeds, black peppercorns, chili powder, turmeric, cloves, and ginger.
2. Stir the mix completely and evenly. Combine in the vinegar and begin to mash everything together into a paste.
3. Place your paste into a jar and seal the lid tightly. Your paste will stay fresh in the fridge for about 3 to 4 weeks.
4. Enjoy.

SIMPLE
Homemade Red / Green Curry Paste (Thailand Style)

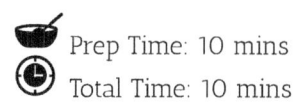

Prep Time: 10 mins
Total Time: 10 mins

Servings per Recipe: 1
Calories   300.4
Fat   3.5 g
Cholesterol   0 mg
Sodium   2368.8 mg
Carbohydrates   71.1 g
Protein   7.5 g

Ingredients

1/4 C. chopped scallion
1/4 C. chopped fresh cilantro
2 tbsps minced garlic
2 tbsps grated fresh gingerroot
1 tbsp freshly grated lemon rinds
1 tbsp brown sugar
1-2 fresh red chilies or 1-2 green chili, minced

3 tbsps fresh lemon juice
1 tbsp ground coriander
1 tsp turmeric
1/2 tsp salt

Directions

1. Add the following your food processor: scallion, cilantro, garlic, ginger root, lemons / lime, brown sugar, chilies, lemon / lime juice, coriander, turmeric, and salt.
2. Process and pulse everything until it becomes a smooth paste.
3. Enjoy.

ENJOY THE RECIPES?
KEEP ON COOKING WITH 6 MORE FREE COOKBOOKS!

Visit our website and simply enter your email address to join the club and receive your 6 cookbooks.

http://booksumo.com/magnet

https://www.instagram.com/booksumopress/

https://www.facebook.com/booksumo/

Printed in Great Britain
by Amazon